Totally Spanish

Classic Spanish Recipes to Make at Home

Sarah Spencer

ISBN: 9781720029793

Printed in the United States

Contents

The Spanish Cuisine

The geography of any country shows in its food, and Spain is no
different. Its miles and miles of ocean coast, lush farmland, and
high and dry mountain terrain give it a wide variety of fresh
foods. In this country you'll find lots of healthy seafood, olive
groves, vineyards, nuts, rice, and a vast array of fruits and
vegetables.

So what do the Spanish make with this rich selection of
ingredients? Well, thanks to the many and varied cultures that
have settled or passed through Spain throughout its long history,
they make a lot of wonderful things. The Greeks brought olives
and olive oil, and the Phoenicians their rich sauces. The Romans
and the French had their influences as well, and then, once ships
started coming back from the New World, there were also
tomatoes, potatoes, vanilla, and chocolate. We see the mark of
the Jewish and Christian populations. However, it was the Moors
who are said to have had the biggest effect on the food of the
region.

The Arabs brought pickling methods, as well as spinach,
sugarcane, rice, apricots and citrus fruits, cinnamon, saffron, and
nutmeg. In fact, their foods tended to be healthier than the foods
we find in the Iberian peninsula where they had less influence.

Because the mountains made travel and communication difficult,
the provinces of the country each have their own specialties and
traditions, but they do have a few things in common: garlic, and
olive oil (lots of it!) In fact, we find what North Americans will no
doubt feel is there is a lot of olive oil in these recipes.

Spain has also, historically, been a poor and mostly rural
country. There are many people who remember growing up with
a diet consisting of a lot of bread, because it was filling. Where

there was food to cook, though, it was fresh, healthy, and simple in terms of both its ingredients and preparation.

Spaniards love their food, and in true Mediterranean fashion, often use mealtimes as an opportunity to come together. From this developed the tradition of *tapas,* now World-wide food tradition to share with friends and family. Tapas are appetizers, or small servings of favorite, usually eaten in company, maybe with a drink or two. Tapas can be as simple as a selection of cured meats and cheese, or they can be fried and decadent.

This collection of recipes has some of the most popular and classic Spanish recipes. The authentic flavors of these recipes will make you truly believe you are eating a meal in good company just like if you were Spain! You will find recipes that are sure to please and surprise your family and friends.

Spanish Pantry Staples

You probably already have many of the things you'll need to prepare Spanish meals, but here are some particularly common things you'll use.

Olive oil
As we have mentioned, olive oil is very common in Spanish cuisine. Choose a Spanish bottle, and it should be high quality, extra virgin. This means you're getting an unrefined oil that is low in acid and (as long as it is reasonably fresh) will have retained its health benefits.

Olives
A favorite alone or as tapas, olives are also used in many recipes. Black and green, canned, flavored, and stuffed – they're all found here.

Garlic
Lots of it, and always fresh.

Paprika
There are many varieties of paprika, but the favorite in Spain is *pimentón*. It comes in various levels of spiciness, but cooks agree that the quality matters.

Saffron
Saffron is the dried stigma of a crocus, and so it's rather expensive. However, you can buy it in small quantities. It's a critical component in many Spanish dishes, especially paella.

Spanish chorizo
It's very important to note that Spanish chorizo is not the same as Mexican. Here, it's a hard sausage spiced with lots of pimentón, and it doesn't require cooking (though we often cook it anyway).

Equipment

In most ways, a Spanish kitchen is the same as any kitchen, anywhere. You'll find knives and cutting boards, pots, and peelers. There are a few things, however, that will make some of the dishes easier to make.

Paella pan

This is a wide, flat pan with two side handles that is (of course) used to make paella – a rice dish commonly made with vegetables and meat or seafood. The advantage in the wide bottom surface is that the rice can cook evenly without stirring, which gives it a less starchy texture. Additionally, once the liquid evaporates, the bottom of the dish becomes crusty and forms what is called a *socarrat*, a caramelized, toasted layer that can make or break the paella experience.

Paella spoon

Because the paella pan is wide and the contents steaming hot, a long-handled spoon is used, to protect the arms and hands from the heat.

Garlic press

So much garlic is used, it's nice to have a quick and tidy way to prepare it.

Clay pots

Unglazed. Spaniards love their stews, and these are traditionally made in a clay pot. The clay is porous, so it allows the heat access to the contents of the pot. Additionally, it is alkaline, and reacts with acidic foods, causing them to develop a deeper, sometimes sweet, flavor. The rustic look and feel of these beautiful pots adds to the experience of the meal as well.

Unglazed clay pots do require some care and consideration. Remember they're used for slow cooking only, and not normally directly on the stovetop. Here are some tips for their use and care.

1. Before you first use the pot, soak it in cold water for up to 2 hours. Dry it out, and then rub the inner surface with a clove of garlic and then olive oil. Fill it three-quarters full with water, and then baked at low temperature for 2–3 hours.
2. Always soak the pot and its lid in cold water for 15 minutes before using. The steam from this moisture will help to cook the food.
3. Your clay pot goes into a cold oven – no preheating! A sudden change in temperature may crack the pot. Similarly, do not pour cold liquid into a hot pot.
4. Hand wash only, and avoid detergents when cleaning your pot. They will soak into the clay and then leech into your food. You can rub any stains with baking soda or a kitchen sponge.

Now that you have an idea of the ingredients and tools you'll need, let's have a look at the recipes themselves!

Tapas Recipes

The Spanish have made an art of snacks and appetizers, and they're called *tapas*. Here are some common (and delicious) recipes you might want to try the next time you're entertaining, or even if you would just like to take a little time to do something special for yourself.

Garlic Shrimp (*Gambas al Ajillo*)

Shrimp in garlic, with a bit of heat.

Servings: 4 - Prep time: 10 min - Cooking time: 10 min

Ingredients
½ cup extra-virgin olive oil
10 large cloves garlic, minced
1 teaspoon red pepper flakes
1 pound shrimp, deveined, shells left on
Juice of 1 lemon
2 ounces Spanish brandy (or dry sherry)
½ teaspoon sweet Spanish paprika
Salt and freshly ground pepper to taste
2 teaspoons fresh parsley leaves (chopped)
1 fresh baguette

Directions
1. Heat the oil in a heavy medium skillet. Add the garlic and red pepper flakes and cook for 1 minute, just until the garlic begins to turn golden.
2. Turn up the heat and add the shrimp, lemon juice, brandy, and paprika. Stir well, and then cook until the shrimp are done, about 3–4 minutes. Remove the skillet from the heat and season with salt and pepper.
3. Remove the shrimp and the seasoned oil to a serving bowl, and sprinkle with parsley. Serve with slices of baguette.

Nutritional information
Calories: 599, Fat: 29.4 g, Protein: 29.3 g,
Carbs: 37.4 g, Sodium: 625.6 mg

Stuffed Tomatoes (*Tamates Rellenos*)

Tomatoes with creamy filling, lovely on a hot afternoon.

Servings: 8 - Prep time: 10 min - Cooking time: 10 sec

Ingredients
8 small tomatoes
4 hard-boiled eggs
⅓ cup garlic aioli (or plain mayonnaise, if desired)
½ teaspoon salt
½ teaspoon black pepper
1 tablespoon parsley, chopped

Directions
1. Peel the tomatoes. Boil a pot of water, and set a bowl of ice water beside it. Carefully remove the cores of the tomatoes with a sharp knife, and cut a shallow x in the bottom.
2. Drop the tomatoes into the boiling water, and leave them for 10 seconds before moving them to the ice water. Carefully remove the skins.
3. If necessary, slice off the bottoms of the tomatoes so they will sit flat, and cut off the tops (reserving those for later).
4. Using a knife and a spoon, carefully remove the insides of the tomatoes.
5. Mash the eggs with the aioli, salt, pepper, and parsley. Spoon the filling back into the tomatoes, and replace the tops at an angle.

Nutritional information
Calories: 125, Fat: 9.8 g, Protein: 4.2 g,
Carbs: 6.1 g , Sodium: 247.7 mg

Shrimp Fritters (*Camarones*, or *Gambas*)

When making these, be sure to keep the oil temperature high so the dough does not absorb too much oil and become soggy.

Servings: 6 - Prep time: 15 min plus 1 h refrigeration - Cooking time: 15 min

Ingredients
½ pound small shrimp, peeled
1 ½ cups chickpea flour
4 teaspoons fresh parsley, chopped
2 scallions, white part and a little of the green, finely chopped
½–1 teaspoon sweet paprika
Dash cayenne pepper
½ teaspoon salt
½ teaspoon black pepper
Extra-virgin olive oil for frying

Directions
1. In a medium saucepan, combine the shrimp with enough water to cover, and place it over high heat. When it comes to a boil, immediately remove the shrimp, cover, and refrigerate. Reserve 1 cup of the cooking water.
2. In a medium bowl, combine the flour, parsley, scallions, paprika, cayenne, salt, and pepper. Pour in the reserved water to make a batter. Refrigerate for 1 hour.
3. Mince the shrimp until it is very fine, almost a paste. Pour in the batter, and mix well.
4. In a thick pan, heat 1 inch of oil until it is almost smoking, to about 375°F. Put the oven on low, and prepare an oven-proof platter with layers of paper towel.
5. Spoon the batter into the oil 1 tablespoon at a time, flattening it with the back of the spoon into a 3-inch circle. Take care not to crowd the pan.

6. Fry for about 1 minute per side, until golden.
7. Remove the fritters with a slotted spoon. Allow the oil to drip back into the pan, and place the fritters on the prepared platter. Keep them in the oven until all the batter is cooked.
8. Before adding more batter to the oil, make sure it has come back up to temperature.

Nutritional information
Calories: 331, Fat: 25.3 g, Protein: 13.4 g,
Carbs: 14.3 g, Sodium: 296.0 mg

Green Olive Hummus

This recipe can be made with canned chickpeas, but taking the time to soak and cook them gives you a much creamier texture.

Servings: 10 - Prep time: 5 min - Cooking time: 4–5 min

Ingredients
2 cups cooked chickpeas (use 1 cup dried, soak overnight, and simmer until tender)
¼ cup tahini
Juice of half a lemon
3 cloves garlic, minced
10 Spanish green olives, pitted
2 tablespoons olive oil, more for drizzling, if desired
½ teaspoon ground cumin
½ teaspoon kosher salt, or to taste

Optional: sliced baguette or multigrain crackers for serving

Directions
1. Combine all the ingredients in a food processor, and combine until smooth.
2. Drizzle with more olive oil, if desired.

Nutritional information
Calories: 130, Fat: 7.5 g , Protein: 3.4 g,
Carbs: 12.3 g , Sodium: 456.8 mg

Roasted Red Pepper and Cilantro Tapenade

This spread is delicious with fresh vegetables, or with pitas.

*Yields about 2 cups - Prep time: 15 min
plus 2 h refrigeration time*

Ingredients

1 cup roasted red peppers, drained and chopped
1 (6 ounce) jar marinated artichoke hearts, drained and chopped
½ cup fresh cilantro, finely chopped
½ cup Parmesan cheese, grated
⅓ cup olive oil
2 tablespoons capers, drained
3 cloves garlic, chopped
1 tablespoon fresh lemon juice
½ teaspoon salt
½ teaspoon pepper

Directions

1. In a food processor, combine all the ingredients and pulse until everything is finely chopped.
2. Transfer the mixture to a serving bowl, cover, and refrigerate for two hours before serving.

Nutritional information

*Calories: 80, Fat: 6.9 g, Protein: 2.1 g,
Carbs: 2.7 g, Sodium: 224 mg*

Catalan Tomato Bread (*Pan con Tomate*)

This very popular snack is sometimes eaten at breakfast, which is the lightest meal of the day in Spain. Like much of Spanish food, it is simplicity itself.

Servings: 10 - Prep time: 10 min - Cooking time: 5 min

Ingredients
1 loaf rustic artisan bread
2–3 cloves garlic
2 large ripe tomatoes
2 tablespoons extra virgin olive oil
Salt

Directions
1. Slice the loaf, discarding the ends, and toast the slices lightly.
2. Peel the garlic and slice off the tip. Rub the cloves on the bread.
3. Slice the tomatoes in half, exposing the juicy center. Rub the cut side on the bread as well.
4. Serve with a drizzle of olive oil and a sprinkle of salt, if desired.

Nutritional information
Calories: 95.6, Fat: 3.0 g, Protein: 2.6 g,
Carbs: 15.4 g, Sodium: 170.3 mg

Curried Sweet Potato Samosas

These tasty little morsels will disappear fast.

Servings: 4 - Prep time: 30 min - Cooking time: 15 min

Ingredients
1 ½ cups sweet potato, mashed
1 teaspoon butter
1 tablespoon milk
4 teaspoons dry onion soup mix
1 teaspoon curry powder
20 wonton wrappers
Sesame oil for brushing

Optional: chutney for serving

Directions
1. Preheat the oven to 375°F and prepare a baking sheet with cooking spray.
2. Combine the sweet potato, butter, milk, soup mix, and curry powder. Mix well.
3. Into each wonton wrapper, spoon a generous teaspoon of filling. Wet the edges, and press them closed. Brush both sides with sesame oil.
4. Arrange the samosas on the baking sheet. Bake for 10 minutes on one side, and then 5 minutes on the other side.

Nutritional information
Calories: 169, Fat: 3 g, Protein: 4.7 g,
Carbs: 30.6 g, Sodium: 332 mg

Ham Croquettes (*Croquetas de Jamón*)

These are a great way to impress your guests and use up that leftover ham. Enjoy these while they are steaming hot.

Servings: 6 - Prep time: 15 min plus 3 h cooling time – Cooking time: 25 min

Ingredients
½ cup olive oil
¾ cup flour
½ cup chicken broth
1 ½ cups milk
½ teaspoon nutmeg
¼ teaspoon black pepper
½ cup ham, minced
2 eggs
2 teaspoons water
1 cup breadcrumbs (for coating)
Spanish olive oil for frying

Directions
1. Heat the ½ cup of olive oil in a medium saucepan. Sift in the flour, and cook for 3–4 minutes, stirring constantly.
2. Gradually add the chicken stock and milk, and continue to cook and stir until it thickens (20–30 minutes).
3. Add the nutmeg, pepper, and ham, and again cook and stir until it is smooth and thick.
4. Allow the mixture to cool, and refrigerate for 3 hours (or overnight) until it is easy to handle.
5. Beat the eggs and water together in a bowl.
6. Pour the breadcrumbs into a separate bowl.
7. With generously floured hands, divide the mixture into 1-inch balls. Set them aside, not touching, until you are ready to fry them.

8. Set out a large platter with a layer of paper towel.
9. In a large, deep pan, heat half an inch of oil to 355°F.
10. Dip the croquettes in the egg and then roll them in the breadcrumbs. Drop them into the oil and cook them quickly, turning often, until they are nicely browned.
11. Set them aside on the lined platter, and let the oil come back up to temperature before adding more croquettes to the pan.
12. Serve immediately!

Nutritional information
Calories: 668, Fat: 60 g, Protein: 8 g,
Carbs: 27 g, Sodium: 526 mg

Stuffed Mussels

(*Mejillones Rellenos*, or *Tigres*)

This dish comes from the north of Spain, where seafood is plentiful.

Servings: 4 - Prep time: 15 min - Cooking time: 30 min

Ingredients

25 mussels, cleaned and debearded
3 tablespoons butter
1 tablespoon olive oil
1 small onion, diced
2 cloves garlic, crushed and minced
Salt and pepper to taste
¼ cup flour
¼ cup white wine
¾ cup 1% milk
2 tablespoons chopped parsley
½ cup Parmesan cheese, shredded

Directions

1. Place the mussels in a pot and cover them with cold water. Place the pot on the stove and bring it to a boil.
2. When the shells are open, remove the pot from the heat; do not overcook. Drain the water and discard any shells that haven't opened.
3. Preheat the oven to 350°F.
4. In a medium skillet, heat the butter and olive oil. Add the onion and garlic, and cook until they are translucent. Season with salt and pepper.
5. Sprinkle the flour over the onion, and let it cook for a few minutes. Gradually stir in the white wine, and then the milk.

6. When the mussels have cooled, remove them from the shell and chop them up, not too small. Set out half the shells on a baking sheet.
7. Add the mussel meat and the parsley to the skillet, and stir.
8. Divide the mixture among the prepared shells, and top each with Parmesan.
9. Bake for about 10 minutes, until the cheese is melted and browned.
10. Serve, and enjoy!

Nutritional information
Calories: 381, Fat: 18 g, Protein: 33 g,
Carbs: 17 g, Sodium: 904 mg

Fried Anchovies (*Boquerones*)

This very popular tapas food that comes from the South of Spain is easy to make at home.

Servings: 4 - Prep time: 20 min - Cooking time: 30 min

Ingredients:
Olive oil for frying (about 3 cups)
3 pounds fresh anchovies, about 60 anchovies
1 ½ cups white flour
1 tablespoon salt
1 teaspoon black pepper
2 lemons, cut into wedges

Directions:
1. Pour the oil into a medium-sized saucepan and place it over medium-high heat.
2. Wash and drain the fish. Using a small knife, cut around the head just below the gills. Gently pull the head away from the fish, so the backbone and innards come away. When the fish are all filleted, rinse and drain them again, and pat them dry.
3. Coat each fish with the flour mixture, and set them aside on a platter, being sure they don't touch.
4. When the oil reaches 360°F, drop the fish in one at a time. Keep the batches small, and cook the fish for about 1 ½ minutes, until they are golden. Set them aside on paper towel to drain, and repeat until all the fish is cooked.
5. Serve hot, with lots of lemon wedges.

Nutritional information
Calories: 527, Fat: 33 g, Protein: 22.5 g,
Carbs: 39.1 g, Sodium: 3946 mg

Chicken Recipes

Paella with Chicken and Chorizo

Paella is mainly known as a seafood dish, but it used to be just...lunch. It's a dish meant to be made with whatever fresh ingredients that are readily available.

Servings: 6 - Prep time: 15 min - Cooking time: 1 h

Ingredients
2 ½ cups fish stock
2 ½ cups chicken stock
½ teaspoon saffron
1 ½ teaspoons smoked Spanish paprika, divided
4 chicken thighs, skin removed
8 ounces chorizo, thinly sliced
½ teaspoon salt
1 tablespoon olive oil
1 medium onion, chopped
½ red bell pepper, chopped
¼ cup chopped parsley
5 cloves garlic, chopped
2 cups Bomba (short grain) rice
½ tomato, chopped
⅓ cup roasted red peppers
6 cloves garlic, peeled

Directions
1. Heat the oven to 350°F.
2. In a medium saucepan, combine the fish stock, chicken stock, saffron, and 1 teaspoon of paprika.
3. Cut the chicken into 1" cubes. Sprinkle them with the salt and the remaining paprika.
4. Heat the olive oil in a medium paella pan. Brown the chicken and the chorizo, and then remove them to a platter, cover, and keep warm.

5. Add the onion, red bell pepper, parsley, and chopped garlic, and sauté for 5 minutes.
6. Add the rice, tomato, and roasted red peppers. Cook until the rice begins to brown.
7. Add the broth, and bring the mixture to a boil. Add the chicken and sausage, embedding them into the rice. Arrange the peeled garlic on top.
8. Bake for 30 minutes, stirring occasionally. After 30 minutes, check to see whether the rice is tender. If not, continue to bake until the dish reaches your desired level of doneness.

Nutritional information
Calories: 520, Fat: 20.0 g, Protein: 24.8 g,
Carbs: 59.6 g, Sodium: 887.3 mg

Spicy Cumin Chicken

This warm and sunny spice blend will knock your socks off.

*Servings: 4 - Prep time: 15 min plus 1 h marinating time –
Cooking time: 20 min*

Ingredients
⅓ cup lime juice
2 teaspoons ground cumin
2 teaspoons turmeric
1 ½ teaspoons coriander
1 teaspoon salt
½ teaspoon red pepper flakes
¼ cup olive oil
4 chicken breasts, about 6 ounces each
2 tablespoons olive oil
2 tablespoons mint leaves

Directions
1. In a medium mixing bowl, combine the lime, cumin, turmeric, coriander, salt, red pepper flakes, and ¼ cup olive oil.
2. Cut the chicken into 1" cubes.
3. Divide the marinade in half. Combine one portion with the chicken, and set it in the fridge for one hour.
4. Heat the remaining olive oil in a medium skillet over medium-high heat.
5. Cook the chicken until it is nicely browned, and then pour the remaining sauce on top. Serve warm, garnished with mint leaves.

Nutritional information
*Calories: 400, Fat: 25.3 g, Protein:42.0 g,
Carbs: 3.6 g, Sodium: 675.7 mg*

Garlic Chicken Thighs with Lemon
(*Pollo al Ajillo*)

This recipe is easy to put together, and so tasty.

Servings: 4 - Prep time: 15 min - Cooking time: 45 min

Ingredients
2 tablespoons extra virgin olive oil
1 red chili pepper
8 chicken thighs
½ teaspoon salt
1 teaspoon black pepper
2 lemons
1 head of garlic
2 tablespoons fresh tarragon
¾ cup white wine
1 cup water

Directions
1. Heat the olive oil in a skillet over medium-high heat. Place the chili pepper (whole) into the oil and cook until it is lightly browned. Set it aside.
2. Rinse the thighs and pat them try with paper towel. Season with salt and pepper, and place them into the hot oil.
3. Cut each lemon into 8 segments and place them into the pan.
4. Peel and crush the garlic cloves, and add them as well, together with the tarragon and the chili pepper.
5. Cook for 3–5 minutes, stirring occasionally, and then add the wine. Continue to cook for a few minutes, and then add the water, lower the heat to medium, and simmer for 30 minutes.

Nutritional information
Calories: 495, Fat: 29.6 g, Protein: 44.1 g,
Carbs: 3.9 g, Sodium: 984.8 mg

Chicken in Almond Sauce
(*Pollo en Pepitoria*)

Rich and satisfying, this recipe is bound to be pleasing to everyone at your table.

Servings: 4 - Prep time: 10 min - Cooking time: 45 min

Ingredients
¼ cup extra virgin olive oil, divided
1 (3 to 3 ½ pounds chicken with the skin attached
1 teaspoon salt
½ teaspoon red pepper flakes
1 onion, diced
2 cups chicken stock
1 cup dry white wine or sherry
1 bay leaf
½ teaspoon cinnamon
4 hard boiled eggs
½ cup raw almonds
4 cloves garlic
Pinch of saffron threads

Directions
1. Heat 3 tablespoons of the olive oil in a skillet over medium-high heat. Season the chicken with salt and red pepper flakes, and place them into the hot oil. Brown them on both sides, and then remove them to a platter.
2. Decrease the heat, and add the onion to the oil. Cook for about 5 minutes, and then return the chicken to the pan. Add the chicken stock and wine, bay leaf, and cinnamon. Cover, and simmer for 25 minutes.

3. In a clean skillet, heat the remaining tablespoon of olive oil. Add the almonds and garlic, and sauté until they are golden brown. Remove them to a blender.
4. Peel the eggs and remove the yolks. Place them in the blender, and reserve the whites for later.
5. Process the almonds, garlic, and egg yolk until smooth, adding a splash of water if needed.
6. Stir this paste into the stew, and add the saffron. Simmer gently until the sauce thickens and the chicken is cooked through. Remove the bay leaf before serving.

Nutritional information
Calories: 1054.2, Fat: 72.9 g, Protein: 76.8 g,
Carbs: 369.6 g, Sodium: 996.4 mg

Pontevedra Chicken

This is a simple and delicious chicken recipe from Andalusia.

Servings: 6 - Prep time: 25 min - Cooking time: 1 h

Ingredients
1 (3 to 3 ½-pound) whole chicken, cut into pieces, skin on
½ cup olive oil
¼ cup butter, melted
1 head roasted garlic, peeled and minced
¼ cup Spanish sweet paprika
1 teaspoon salt
½ teaspoon crushed red pepper flakes

Directions
1. Preheat the oven to 350°F.
2. Arrange the chicken pieces in a baking dish, and pour the oil and butter over them. Place them skin side down.
3. Sprinkle with the minced garlic, paprika, salt, and red pepper flakes.
4. Using clean hands (wear kitchen gloves if you have them) massage the oil and spices into the surface of the chicken.
5. Bake for 30 minutes, and then turn the chicken over. Bake another 30 minutes, until the skin is crispy.
6. Serve with pan sauce on the side.

Nutritional information
Calories: 544.5, Fat: 39.2 g, Protein: 44.7 g,
Carbs: 4.7 g, Sodium: 835.4 mg

Fish and Seafood Recipes

Fish Stew (*Suquet*)

You'll need to make a trip to the seafood market when you make this, but it's worth it! You can vary the fish types and amounts to your liking.

Servings: 6 - Prep time: 2 min - Cooking time: 45 min

Ingredients
18 clams
1 tablespoon sea salt
½ cup olive oil
3 cloves garlic, peeled
¼ cup blanched almonds, whole
1 tablespoon chopped fresh flat-leaf parsley
1 tablespoon water
1 yellow onion, diced
1 tomato, peeled and roughly chopped
Pinch of saffron threads
6 cups fish stock
2 pounds monkfish, chopped
1 pound hake, chopped
6 large shrimp (in the shell)
12 medium shrimp, peeled
½ pound mussels, scrubbed and debearded
½ cup white wine

Directions
1. Scrub the clams and place them in a large bowl. Cover with cold water and sprinkle in the salt, stirring to dissolve. Leave them for 1–2 hours, so they release any sand in their shells.
2. In a large Dutch oven, heat the oil and brown the garlic. When it is golden, remove it to a mortar or a blender, and add the almonds, parsley, and water. Grind or process the mixture into a paste.

3. Return the oil in the pot to the burner over medium, and add the onion. Cook until it begins to soften, and then stir in the tomato and saffron.
4. In a separate saucepan, warm the fish stock until it simmers.
5. Add the monkfish, hake, and shrimp to the pot, and stir in one cup of the hot broth. Add another cup of broth every 5 minutes, stirring each time.
6. Drain and rinse the clams and add them to the stew, together with the garlic mixture, mussels, and the wine. Cover, and cook for 5–10 minutes, until the shells open. Discard any clams or mussels that don't open.
7. Serve immediately.

Nutritional information
Calories: 541, Fat: 26.3 g, Protein: 78.0 g,
Carbs: 9.2 g, Sodium: 1013.5 mg

Spanish Fish Curry

Servings: 4 - Prep time: 10 min - Cooking time: 40 min

Ingredients
4 mackerel fillets, about 1" thick
½ teaspoon salt
3 tablespoons curry powder
¼ cup olive oil
1 thumb fresh ginger root, finely sliced
4 cloves garlic, minced
3 shallots, thinly sliced
2 cardamom pods
1 cinnamon stick
2 curry leaf stalks
1 ½ tablespoons dried red pepper flakes
1 ½ cups coconut milk, diluted in 3 cups of water
6 pickled green olives, drained and rinsed
3 green chilies

Directions
1. Clean the fish and season it with the salt, set it aside.
2. Combine the curry powder with just enough water to make a paste and set it aside.
3. Heat the olive oil in a large saucepan, and add the ginger, garlic, and shallots. Sauté for 3–4 minutes.
4. Add the cardamom pods and cinnamon, and stir in the curry paste.
5. Stir the curry leaves and the red pepper flakes.
6. Add a few tablespoons of water and continue to cook for 3–4 minutes, adding more water if necessary to prevent it from drying out.
7. Pour in the coconut milk and the olives, and stir to combine.

8. Add the fish pieces, turning them to coat with the hot sauce. Simmer for 5–8 minutes to allow the fish to cook, stirring carefully as necessary.
9. Turn off the heat, and add the green chilies. Let it rest for 5 minutes before serving.

Nutritional information
Calories: 421, Fat: 32.4 g, Protein: 22.6 g,
Carbs: 10.0 g, Sodium: 496.9 mg

Paella

We can't talk about Spanish cuisine – especially seafood – without including paella! The trick to this dish is to cook it in a paella pan if you can (or a large skillet if you must) and *do not stir the rice while it's cooking.*

Servings: 6 - Prep time: 10 min - Cooking time: 30 min

Ingredients
2 tablespoons olive oil
3 cloves garlic, minced
1 large onion, diced
1 red bell pepper, diced
1 large tomato, peeled and diced (with juice and seeds)
8 ounces chicken thigh fillets, chopped
6 ounces calamari, cut into thin rings
1 ½ cups paella rice
3 ½ cups chicken broth
1 teaspoon saffron threads
12–16 large prawns, whole (shell on)
12 large mussels
Lemon wedges for serving

Directions
1. Heat the oil in the pan and cook the garlic and onion until they begin to soften, about 5 minutes. Add the bell pepper and cook for another few minutes, and then stir in the tomato.
2. Add the chicken and calamari, and cook until they are lightly browned.
3. Add the rice, and stir until it is covered in oil. Add the broth and stir in the saffron very briefly.

4. Heat until the liquid boils, simmer for a few minutes, and then reduce the heat to medium low. Cook for 7 minutes. The rice will be near the surface of the liquid, but not dry.
5. Press the prawns into the rice until they are mostly submerged, and then do the same with the mussels. Don't stir.
6. Cook for an additional 5–8 minutes, until the prawns are cooked through and the mussel shells are opened. (Discard any that don't open.)
7. Test the rice for doneness, adding more water and cooking a little longer if necessary.
8. Let stand for 5 minutes, garnish with lemon, and serve.

Nutritional information
Calories: 422, Fat: 12.6 g, Protein: 35.4 g,
Carbs: 22.0 g, Sodium: 1184.2 mg

Spanish Seafood Stew (*Caldereta*)

Try this recipe from the north coast.

Servings: 4 - Prep time: 35 min - Cooking time: 1 h

Ingredients
¼ cup olive oil
1 onion, finely chopped
1 red bell pepper, seeded and diced
6 cloves garlic, finely chopped
2 cups chopped tomatoes
2 cups white wine
3 cups water
½ cup garlic mayonnaise (aioli)
1 teaspoon sweet paprika
¾ cup brandy
1 ½ pounds skinless firm white fish fillets, cut in bite-sized chunks
16 prawns, peeled (tails intact), deveined
12 scallops
½ cup parsley, finely chopped
Crusty bread, to serve

Directions
1. Heat the oil in a skillet over medium heat and add the onion and pepper. Stir-fry for 5–8 minutes, until softened. Add the garlic and cook for 2 more minutes.
2. Stir in the tomatoes and let them simmer for 10 minutes. Stir in the wine and water and bring the pot to a boil. Reduce the heat to simmer, and cook for 20 minutes.
3. In a small mixing bowl, combine the garlic mayo and paprika. Set aside.
4. In a separate saucepan, heat the brandy and cook off some of the alcohol, 2–3 minutes.

5. Add the brandy and fish to the soup, and cook for 2–3 minutes before stirring in the prawns and scallops. Simmer for an additional 2–3 minutes, until the seafood is cooked.
6. Garnish with parsley, and serve with bread and aioli.

Nutritional information
Calories: 842, Fat: 36.9 g, Protein: 54.7 g,
Carbs: 29.6 g, Sodium: 594.2 mg

Roasted Monkfish with Piperade Sauce

Monkfish, sometimes called "poor man's lobster," is a mildly flavored fish that can be prepared in a variety of ways.

Servings: 4 - Prep time: 20 min - Cooking time: 40 min

Ingredients

2 pounds monkfish tail on the bone
5 tablespoons extra virgin olive oil, divided
3 cloves garlic, minced, divided
1 red onion, finely sliced
1 tablespoon chili, deseeded and minced
2 red bell peppers, finely sliced
2 green bell peppers, finely sliced
½ cup dry white wine
4 large, ripe tomatoes, diced
1 bay leaf
2 sprigs thyme
1 teaspoon sea salt
¼ teaspoon black pepper
¼ cup parsley, chopped

Directions

1. Rinse the fish under cold running water, removing all remaining skin and tissue.
2. In a small mixing bowl, combine 1 tablespoon of olive oil and 2 teaspoons minced garlic, and rub this all over the fish.
3. In a saucepan, heat 2 tablespoons of oil over medium heat and cook the rest of the garlic for 1–2 minutes. Add the onion, chili pepper, and bell peppers, and cook to soften.

4. Stir in the wine and cook for another few minutes to let it reduce slightly, and then add the tomatoes, bay leaf, and thyme. Simmer on low for 20 minutes.
5. Preheat the oven to 400°F.
6. In a Dutch oven (or ovenproof pan) heat the remaining oil and brown the fish on all sides. Season with salt and pepper.
7. Pour the sauce over the fish, and turn to coat.
8. Roast in the preheated oven for 10 minutes, basting and turning halfway through.
9. Sprinkle with parsley, and serve.

Nutritional information
Calories: 472, Fat: 22.2 g, Protein: 45.2 g,
Carbs: 18.8 g, Sodium: 657.0 mg

Shrimp Cakes (*Tortillitas de Camarones*)

This is a common street food in Cádiz. They're delicious and easy to make!

*Servings: 5 (10 cakes) - Prep time: 10 min –
Cooking time: 10 min*

Ingredients
2 cups olive oil
1 cup all-purpose flour
½ cup chickpea flour
1 teaspoon salt
2 cups ice water
8 ounces shrimp
2 green onions, finely chopped
2 tablespoons fresh parsley, finely chopped

Directions
1. Heat the oil in a skillet to 365°F.
2. In a mixing bowl, combine the all-purpose flour with the chickpea flour, and mix in the salt.
3. Slowly add the water and mix to form a batter.
4. Add the shrimp, green onions, and parsley, and stir to combine.
5. Ladle some batter into the hot oil and cook on both sides until golden. Drain on paper towel, and serve.

Nutritional information
*Calories: 221, Fat: 7.6 g, Protein: 14.1 g,
Carbs: 23.5 g, Sodium: 23.5 mg*

Beef Recipes

Stewed Short Ribs (*Estofado de Catalana*)

A *gremolata* is a seasoned herb mixture that we use to garnish a dish. Try one with these tender short ribs! Make this dish when you have lots of time.

Servings: 8 - Prep time: 20 min - Cook time: 3–4 h

Ingredients
For the ribs
6 pounds beef short ribs
¼ cup olive oil
Salt and pepper to taste
2 large yellow onions, diced
2 carrots, peeled and sliced
2 stalks celery, diced
4 cloves garlic, crushed and minced
2 cups red wine
½ cup tomato paste
1 cup canned plum tomatoes, cut into chunks
2 ½ quarts low-sodium beef stock
2 sprigs fresh thyme

For the sauce
2 cups dry sherry
2 tablespoons cocoa powder
1 teaspoon dried thyme
1 teaspoon dried marjoram
2 tablespoons orange zest, finely grated
2 tablespoons butter

For the gremolata
1 teaspoon orange zest, finely grated
¼ cup fresh parsley, minced
Extra virgin olive oil

Salt and pepper to taste

Mashed potatoes or rice for serving

Directions
1. Preheat the oven to 300°F.
2. Sprinkle the ribs generously with salt and pepper. Heat the olive oil in large a Dutch oven. Working in batches, brown the ribs until they are golden. Set them aside.
3. In the pot, cook the onions, carrots, celery, and garlic until caramelized, about 10–15 minutes.
4. Stir in the wine and simmer, stirring often, until the wine reduces by half.
5. Add the tomato paste, tomatoes, beef stalk, and thyme sprigs. Add the ribs, and bring the mixture to a boil.
6. Cover, and move the pot to the oven. Cook for 3 ½ hours, until the meat is very tender.
7. After baking, strain the sauce well and place it in a large saucepan. Stir in the sherry and simmer until the sauce is reduced by half.
8. Add the cocoa, thyme, marjoram, orange zest, and butter. Taste, and add salt and pepper to your liking.
9. When the sauce is warmed through, add the ribs and stir to coat.
10. To make the gremolata, combine the orange zest and parsley, and add a few drops of olive oil to moisten. Season with salt and pepper.
11. To plate the meal, place half a cup of potato or rice in the dish. Top with a few ribs, a drizzle of sauce, and a sprinkle of gremolata.

Nutritional information
Calories: 1085, Fat: 66.5 g, Protein: 70.7 g,
Carbs: 33.0 g, Sodium: 2029.6 mg

Beef and Cheese Empanadas

These can be served as tapas, or as a main meal with a side of salad.

Makes: 20 - Prep time: 15 min plus cooling time –
Cook time: 45–50 min

Ingredients

1 pound lean ground beef
1 tablespoon chili powder
1 teaspoon ground cumin
1 teaspoon salt
½ teaspoon black pepper
¼ teaspoon red pepper flakes
1 green bell pepper, diced
1 red bell pepper, diced
1 small onion, diced
4 cloves garlic, minced
½ cup mushrooms, diced
1 (10 ounce) can diced tomatoes
1 large egg, beaten
¼ cup grated Romano cheese
1 cup cheddar cheese, shredded
2 teaspoons olive oil
20 prepared empanada pastry rounds (thawed)
1 large egg beaten with 1 teaspoon water
2 tablespoons grated Romano cheese

Directions

1. In a skillet over medium-high heat, brown the beef and drain the grease.
2. Add the chili powder, cumin, salt, black pepper, and red pepper flakes. Mix well.
3. Add the green and red pepper, onion, garlic, mushrooms, and stewed tomatoes. Simmer until most of the liquid has evaporated, about 5 minutes.
4. Add the beaten egg and mix well.
5. Remove the skillet from the heat and stir in the cheeses. Allow the mixture to cool completely.
6. Preheat the oven to 375°F, and prepare a baking sheet with cooking spray.
7. To assemble the empanadas, lay out one wrapper and brush the inside edges with egg wash.
8. Scoop a generous tablespoon of filling into the center of the wrapper. Fold the pastry over, and seal the edges with a fork.
9. Arrange the filled empanadas on the baking tray. Brush the tops with olive oil, and sprinkle with the remaining Romano cheese.
10. Bake for about 20–25 minutes, until they are hot and golden brown.

Nutritional information

Calories: 209, Fat: 13.0 g, Protein: 8.2 g,
Carbs: 14.6 g, Sodium: 442.4 mg

Spanish Ox Tail Stew (*Rabo de Toro*)

A rich and hearty stew from the south of Spain.

Servings: 4 - Prep time: 10 min - Cook time: 3 h, 15 min

Ingredients
3 tablespoons olive oil
4 pounds ox or beef tails
½ teaspoon salt
½ teaspoon freshly ground black pepper
¼ cup flour
3 carrots, sliced
1 large sweet onion, diced
1 red pepper, diced
2 ripe tomatoes, diced
4 cloves garlic, crushed and minced
1 bay leaf
2 cloves
1 teaspoon ground ginger
3 cups beef stock
2 cups red wine

Optional: French fries for serving

Directions
1. In a Dutch oven, heat the olive oil until it shimmers.
2. In a bowl, season the ox tails with salt and pepper and sprinkle them with flour. Toss to coat, and discard any excess flour.
3. Working in batches, sear the ox tails in the oil, removing them as they are well browned. Cover, and set aside.
4. In the pot, combine the carrots, onion, red pepper, tomatoes, and garlic.

5. Add the bay leaf, cloves, and ginger, and cook for 2 minutes.
6. Add the meat back to the pot, and pour in the beef stock and wine.
7. Bring the mixture to a boil, then lower the heat to simmer. Cover, and cook for about 3 hours.
8. When the meat is tender, remove the sauce to a blender and purée until smooth. Pour it back over the meat.
9. Serve over French fries, if desired, and enjoy!

Nutritional information
Calories: 560, Fat: 24.5 g, Protein: 57.9 g,
Carbs: 27.2 g, Sodium: 881 mg

Catalan Beef Stew with Wine and Cinnamon
(*Estofado de Ternara a la Catalana*)

This rich stew has a surprise ingredient: chocolate! Serve with hot white rice.

Servings: 6 - Prep time: 10 min - Cook time: 1 ½ h

Ingredients
¼ cup Spanish olive oil
2 pounds stewing beef, cubed
2 tablespoons flour
1 cup red wine
4 cloves garlic, halved
1 large onion, diced
1 cup diced tomatoes, canned
1 carrot, sliced
1 stalk celery, sliced
1 ounce unsweetened baking chocolate, chopped
¼ teaspoon cinnamon
1 teaspoon salt
½ teaspoon black pepper
½ teaspoon dried thyme
2 cups beef stock
½ cup green onion, chopped

Hot white rice, for serving.

Directions
1. Heat the olive oil in a Dutch oven. Working in batches, cook the stew meat until it is nicely browned.
2. Place all the meat back in the pot, and sprinkle it with the flour.
3. Stir in the wine, and cook for 1–2 minutes. Add the garlic, onion, tomatoes, carrot, and celery.

4. Stir in the chocolate, cinnamon, salt, pepper, thyme, and beef stock. Cover, and simmer for 1 ½ hours, or until the meat is tender.
5. Serve with hot white rice, garnished with green onion.

Nutritional information

Calories: 618, Fat: 29.3 g, Protein: 50 g,
Carbs: 31.3 g, Sodium: 540 mg

Spanish Ground Beef (*Picadillo*)

Picadillo is often served with rice and beans.

Servings: 4 - Prep time: 10 min - Cook time: 25 min

Ingredients
1 pound lean ground beef
4 slices bacon, chopped
1 small onion, diced
½ small green bell pepper, diced
1 teaspoon oregano
1 teaspoon garlic powder
1 teaspoon salt
½ teaspoon black pepper
¼ cup green olives, sliced
1 teaspoon ground cumin
1 teaspoon paprika
½ teaspoon coriander
1 cup tomato sauce

Optional: rice and beans, for serving

Directions
1. Place a large skillet over medium-high heat and add the ground beef. Break it up with the spatula and cook until it begins to brown. Drain the grease.
2. Add all the other ingredients and mix well. Cook for 20 minutes, stirring often.

Nutritional information
Calories: 388, Fat: 28.4 g, Protein: 23.6 g,
Carbs: 9.1 g, Sodium: 1241.7 mg

Pork Recipes

Andalusian Stew (*Olla Podrida*)

This spicy stew's name translates to *rotten pot*, but we promise that it tastes better than it sounds.

Serves: 10 - Prep time: 30 min - Cook time: 5 h

Ingredients

3 cups dried chickpeas, soaked in cold water overnight and drained
1 ½ pounds oxtails
½ pound prosciutto, or ham, cubed
1 ham bone
5 cups cold water, divided
2 cloves garlic, peeled
4 black peppercorns
Pinch of saffron threads, crumbled
½ teaspoon cumin seeds
2 ripe plum tomatoes, peeled and seeded, 1 whole and 1 finely chopped
½ pound green beans, ends trimmed and chopped
8–10 chicken legs
1 pound mild Italian sausage (or Spanish chorizo, which is not as spicy as Mexican)
1 large yellow potato, such as Yukon gold
Salt to taste

Directions

1. Put the chickpeas into a large soup pot with the oxtail, prosciutto or ham, and the ham bone. Add 4 cups of the cold water. Bring it to a simmer slowly and then cook for 1 hour, skimming the foam off from time to time.
2. Meanwhile, in a mortar, pound the garlic, peppercorns, saffron, and cumin together until a mushy mixture is formed. Add the whole tomato and continue pounding

until well combined. (Alternatively, you can do this in a blender or food processor.)

3. Add the green beans, chicken legs, chorizo, potato, and the   chopped tomato to the pot. Stir in the remaining cup of cold water. Stir in the prepared spice mixture and blend well.

4. Cook over very low heat for 2–4 hours, checking from time to time to see how it's coming along. The *cocido* is done when the meat is falling off the chicken legs and the potato has lost its crunch, but before it begins to fall apart. Taste and adjust the seasoning.

Nutritional information
Calories: 640, Fat: 29.8 g, Protein: 55.0 g,
Carbs: 35.9 g, Sodium: 1285 mg

Spanish Roasted Pork (*Pernil*)

This juicy, crispy pork is sure to be a favorite, as it is a traditional recipe in countless Spanish homes.

Serves: 16 - Prep time: 10 min - Cook time: 5 ½ h

Ingredients
9 pounds skin-on, bone-in pork shoulder (picnic) roast
1 lime, halved
10 cloves garlic
2 tablespoons salt
1 ½ tablespoons olive oil, divided
1 tablespoon dried oregano
1 teaspoon ground black pepper
1 ½ teaspoons adobo seasoning
1 teaspoon vinegar
½ teaspoon sazon seasoning
2 cans or bottles beer

Directions
1. Preheat the oven to 350°F. Rinse the pork and pat it dry with a paper towel, and set it in a roasting pan.
2. Rub the lime all over the pork.
3. Mash the garlic into a paste, and mix in the salt, 1 tablespoon oil, oregano, black pepper, adobo seasoning, and vinegar.
4. Peel the skin off the pork to within about 2 inches from the bone, and make small slits all over the pork. Press the seasoned garlic into the slits, and re-cover the meat with the skin.
5. In a small mixing bowl, combine the olive oil with the sazon seasoning, and spread it over the skin.
6. Pour the beer into the pan around the meat, and cover it with foil, sealing the edges well. Roast for about 3 hours.

7. Remove the foil, and increase the oven temperature to 375°F. Cook for an additional 2 ½ hours, until the skin is golden and crispy and the meat is cooked through. Rest for 15 minutes before carving.

Nutritional information
Calories: 362, Fat: 25.2 g, Protein: 26.4 g,
Carbs: 3 g, Sodium: 821 mg

Pork Chops in Fresh Tomato Salsa
(*Chuletas de Puerco en Salsa*)

In this recipe, basic ingredients combine to make a nutritious and delicious meal.

Serves: 4 - Prep time: 15 min - Cook time: 50 min

Ingredients
4 bone-in pork chops
1 teaspoon salt
½ teaspoon black pepper
1 teaspoon garlic powder
½ teaspoon cumin
2 tablespoons olive oil
1 large white onion, thinly sliced, divided
4 large Roma tomatoes quartered
2 serrano chiles, roughly chopped
2 cloves garlic, crushed
½ teaspoon oregano
⅔ cup water
Salt, pepper, garlic powder, cumin to taste
Cilantro for garnish, optional

Hot rice and vegetables for serving

Directions
1. Season the pork chops on both sides with salt, pepper, garlic powder, and cumin.
2. Heat the olive oil in a large skillet over medium heat, and brown the pork chops on both sides.
3. In a blender, combine a quarter of the onion with the tomatoes, serrano peppers, garlic, oregano, and water.
4. Remove the chops to a platter and cover them.

5. Add the remaining onion to the skillet and sauté until it begins to soften, 3–4 minutes.
6. Pour the sauce into the hot skillet and simmer for 8–10 minutes, until it is reduced and thickened. Taste, and adjust the seasonings.
7. Add the pork back to the skillet, cover, and simmer for 30 minutes.
8. Garnish with cilantro if desired, and serve with rice and vegetables.

Nutritional information
Calories: 287, Fat: 16.2 g, Protein: 25.4 g,
Carbs: 8.3 g, Sodium: 645 mg

Pork and Bean Stew (*Fabada Asturiana*)

This is a rich stew that is eaten all around Spain, especially in the winter.

Serves: 6 - Prep time: 20 min plus soaking overnight – Cook time: 3 h

Ingredients
1 pound dried fava beans, soaked overnight in water to cover
2 tablespoons extra virgin olive oil
1 pinch saffron thread
2 teaspoons Spanish smoked paprika
8 cloves garlic
1 ham hock
½ pound bacon
½ pound Spanish chorizo
½ pound blood sausage (or black pudding)
1 small onion, halved

Directions
1. Drain the beans and place them in a stock pot, adding water to cover by 2 inches. Add the olive oil, saffron, paprika, garlic, ham hock, and bacon.
2. Bring it to a boil and lower the heat to simmer. Cook for one hour, skimming from time to time. Add more water if necessary to keep the beans covered.
3. Add the chorizo, sausage, and onion, and simmer for 2 more hours, until the beans are very soft. Add more water as necessary.
4. Remove the pot from the heat, and scoop out the meats. Take any meat off the ham bone, and cut it into bite-sized pieces. Slice the chorizo and sausage. Discard the onion and garlic.

5. Scoop the beans into bowls, and arrange the meats on top. Serve!

Nutritional information
Calories: 369, Fat: 27 g, Protein: 22.6 g,
Carbs: 10.3 g, Sodium: 1045.8 mg

Spanish Ratatouille (*Pisto Manchengo*)

This colorful dish made with fresh vegetables feeds a crowd!

Serves: 10 - Prep time: 10 min - Cook time: 50 min

Ingredients
2 tablespoons olive oil
8 ounces Spanish chorizo, diced
8 ounces ham, diced
1 medium red onion, unpeeled
3 bell peppers, red or green (or mixed)
2 pounds tomatoes, peeled and chopped
2 medium zucchini
1 teaspoon dried oregano
⅛ teaspoon cumin
⅛ teaspoon red pepper flakes

Directions
1. Heat the oil in a large saucepan, and cook the chorizo and ham over low heat. Set them aside.
2. Add the onion and bell peppers, and cook for about 10 minutes, until softened.
3. Stir in the tomatoes and zucchini, and season with oregano, cumin, and red pepper flakes.
4. Cover, and simmer for 30 minutes, until the vegetables are cooked and tender. Add the chorizo and ham, and heat through.
5. Serve immediately.

Nutritional information
Calories: 196, Fat: 12.4 g, Protein: 10.9 g,
Carbs: 10.5 g, Sodium: 474 mg

Vegetarian and Side Recipes

Gazpacho

This is a traditional, fresh, cold soup, bursting with fresh flavor and very nutritious. It's so easy to make!

Serves: 12 - Prep time: 20 min - Cook time: 20 min

Ingredients
2 red bell peppers, roughly chopped
2 medium cucumbers, peeled and roughly chopped
8 ripe tomatoes, roughly chopped
1 large clove garlic (optional)
1 ½ cups water
½ cup extra virgin olive oil
¼ cup apple cider vinegar
½ teaspoon salt
¼ cup plain bread crumbs
Croutons, for serving

Directions
1. Combine all the ingredients EXCEPT the croutons in a blender, and pulse until smooth.
2. Run the soup through a strainer to take out any seeds or bits of skin.
3. Chill for 2–3 hours.
4. Serve with croutons.

Nutritional information
Calories: 259, Fat: 12.6 g, Protein: 26.5 g,
Carbs: 8.2 g, Sodium: 739.4 mg

Salt Cod Salad (*Esqueixada*)

Use salt cod in this easy and light salad from the Catalan region.

Serves: 4 - Prep time: 15 min plus 2–4 h refrigeration –
Cook time: 0 min

Ingredients
1 pound salt cod, soaked and rinsed well
1 yellow onion, thinly sliced
½ teaspoon black pepper
1 cup extra virgin olive oil
2 tomatoes, diced
½ red bell pepper, seeded and diced
½ green pepper, seeded and diced
¼ cup black olives
½ cup white wine vinegar

Directions
1. Tear the cod into bite-sized pieces and place it in a medium-sized mixing bowl. Remove any bits of skin or bones.
2. Add the onion, season with black pepper, and pour in enough oil to cover the mixture.
3. Cover and refrigerate for 1–3 hours.
4. Drain the oil, and move the cod and onion to a clean bowl. Add the tomato, red and green pepper, and olives, and mix well.
5. Drizzle with vinegar, and toss to coat.
6. Keep refrigerated and serve cold.

Nutritional information
Calories: 259, Fat: 12.6 g, Protein: 26.5 g,
Carbs: 8.2 g, Sodium: 739 mg

Escudella

This is a noodle soup with meatballs, from the Catalan region.

Serves: 6 - Prep time: 20 min - Cook time: 1 ½ h

Ingredients
For the meatballs:
8 ounces ground beef
1 egg
2 cloves garlic
2 tablespoons parsley chopped
¼ cup bread crumbs
2 tablespoons flour
2 tablespoons pine nuts

For the broth:
¾ cup chickpeas, soaked in water overnight
6 cups water
1 tablespoon salt
1 beef bone
1 pork bone
1 pound chicken pieces with bones
1 white sausage (such as plain pork)
1 black sausage
1 ½ cups pasta (shells or similar)
2 potatoes, peeled and diced

Directions
1. Drain the chickpeas and place them in a stock pot. Cover with 6 cups of water and 1 tablespoon of salt. Add the beef and pork bones, together with the chicken pieces.
2. Bring the pot to a boil, and lower the heat to simmer over medium-low heat for about an hour.

3. Prepare the meatballs. Combine all the meatball ingredients in a mixing bowl, and combine them with your hands. Shape them into balls and set them aside.
4. Remove the bones and chicken pieces from the broth, and set them aside on a cutting board.
5. Add the meatballs to the broth, together with the sausages, pasta, and potatoes.
6. Shred the meat from the chicken bones and add it back to the pot. Add more water if there is not enough broth.
7. Simmer for half an hour, and season with salt and pepper to your liking.

Nutritional information
Calories: 471, Fat: 16.9 g, Protein: 32.6 g,
Carbs: 45.8 g, Sodium: 1398.4 mg

Spanish Rice

American families all have their own recipe for potato salad, and Spanish families all have their own way to make Spanish rice.

Serves: 6 - Prep time: 10 min - Cook time: 30–40 min

Ingredients
6 tablespoons butter
2 onions, chopped
1 jalapeño pepper, minced*
1 cup uncooked white rice
1 teaspoon salt
½ teaspoon black pepper
2 (14.5 ounce) cans diced tomatoes, undrained
½ cup sour cream, or as desired (optional)
½ cup shredded cheddar cheese, or as desired (optional)

*substitute ¼ cup canned green chilies for milder version

Directions
1. Melt the butter in medium skillet, and add the onion and jalapeño pepper. Stir and cook to soften, about 3 minutes.
2. Add the rice, and cook until it begins to brown, but don't allow it to burn. Season with salt and pepper.
3. Stir in the tomatoes, and bring the mixture to a boil. Reduce the heat to simmer, and cover.
4. Cook for 20–30 minutes, lifting the lid to check and stir the rice from time to time. If it is drying out, add ½ cup of water.
5. Serve garnished with sour cream and cheddar, if desired.

Nutritional information
Calories: 304, Fat: 18.7 g, Protein: 6.1 g,
Carbs: 28.7 g, Sodium: 856.4 mg

Spinach and Chickpeas
(*Espinacas con Carbanzos*)

Try this healthy side dish, packed with fiber and nutrients!

Serves: 6 - Prep time: 5 min - Cook time: 15 min

Ingredients
1 tablespoon extra virgin olive oil
10 cloves garlic, peeled and chopped
2 tablespoons sweet paprika
¼ teaspoon red pepper flakes
6 cups fresh spinach
½ teaspoon sea salt (optional)
½ cup water
3 ½ cups cooked or canned chickpeas

Directions
1. Heat the olive oil in a skillet over medium heat and cook the garlic until fragrant and golden.
2. Add the paprika and spinach, and season with salt, if using. Add the water, and cook for 5 minutes, stirring often.
3. Add the chickpeas, and cook for 5 more minutes.

Nutritional information
Calories: 188, Fat: 2.0 g, Protein: 8.5 g,
Carbs: 35.7 g, Sodium: 637.7 mg

Patatas Bravas

These crisp potato cubes are a big favorite for tapas or as part of a meal.

Servings: 4 - Prep time: 15 min - Cooking time: 45 min

Ingredients
4 large potatoes, peeled and cut in 1" cubes
2 cups olive oil
1 ½ tablespoons salt
1 medium onion, diced
2 cloves garlic, minced
2 red chilies
1 teaspoon smoked paprika
3 cups tomatoes, drained
½ cup mayonnaise

Directions
1. Place the potatoes and the oil in a large, cold skillet and place them over medium heat. Cook until the potatoes are softened, about 12–15 minutes.
2. Turn the heat up to medium-high, and cook until the potatoes are golden. Remove them to a plate lined with paper towel to drain.
3. Remove all but 5 tablespoons of the oil from the skillet, and add the onion. Cook for 2–3 minutes, and then add the garlic, chilies, and paprika. Cook for another 3–4 minutes and then stir in the tomatoes.
4. Simmer for a few minutes, and then transfer the mixture to a blender and process until smooth.
5. Serve the potatoes hot with the tomato sauce and mayonnaise for dipping.

Nutritional information
Calories: 587, Fat: 44.3 g, Protein: 5.9 g,
Carbs: 45.1 g, Sodium: 2804.9 mg

Traditional Bread Soup (*Sopa de Ajo*)

We're betting you've never had anything like this before. This recipe honors the simplicity that marks so much of Spain's traditional cooking.

Serves: 4 - Prep time: 5 min - Cook time: 15 min

Ingredients
½ cup extra-virgin olive oil
8 ounces dense white bread, stale (or use what you have), sliced or torn in pieces
4 cloves garlic, sliced
3 teaspoons paprika (use good quality, whatever variety you like)
6 cups water or vegetable stock
4 eggs (optional)

Directions
1. Heat the olive oil in a skillet over medium heat and cook the garlic until fragrant and golden. Remove it with a slotted spoon before it begins to burn.
2. Place the bread pieces in the oil, and cook until they begin to brown.
3. Remove the pot from the heat and add the paprika, stirring until the bread is well coated. Add the water or stock together with the cooked garlic, and put the pot back on the heat.
4. Cook for 10–15 minutes, stirring occasionally, until you reach the consistency you like.
5. Remove the pot from the heat and crack in the eggs. Let them poach, and then serve.

Nutritional information
Calories: 471, Fat: 34.8 g, Protein: 11.9 g,
Carbs: 30.1 g, Sodium: 350 mg

Spanish Omelet (*Tortilla de Patatas*)

This can be served as tapas, as an entrée, or as a side. It's tasty in all three categories.

Serves: 6 - Prep time: 5 min - Cook time: 15 min

Ingredients
¼ cup olive oil, divided
4 large potatoes, peeled and sliced
1 onion, diced
6 large eggs
Salt and black pepper to taste

Directions
1. Heat half the olive oil in a skillet over medium heat, and cook the potatoes until they are tender. Season with salt and pepper.
2. In a medium mixing bowl, beat the eggs. Add the potatoes and the onion to the eggs, and stir to combine.
3. Tip the mixture back into the skillet, and cook over medium-low heat until the bottom browns.
4. Place a plate over the skillet, and flip the tortilla onto it. Pour the remaining olive oil into the skillet, and slide the tortilla back in to cook on the other side.
5. Season with salt and pepper as desired.

Nutritional information
Calories: 331, Fat: 14.0 g, Protein: 10.7 g,
Carbs: 41.3 g, Sodium: 304.7 mg

Grilled Vegetable Salad (*Escalivada*)

This can be served as tapas, as an entrée, or as a side. It's tasty in all three categories.

Serves: 4 - Prep time: 10 min plus 1 h cooling –
Cook time: 30 min

Ingredients
2 eggplants, halved
1 small red onion, halved
2 red bell peppers, halved and cored
2 tomatoes
⅓ cup extra virgin olive oil, plus some for brushing
3 cloves garlic, thinly sliced
½ teaspoon salt
Pinch red pepper flakes

Directions
1. Preheat the oven to 500°F.
2. Brush the vegetables with oil and arrange them on a baking sheet.
3. Roast the vegetables until they begin to blacken, turning them from time to time, about half an hour.
4. When the vegetables are ready, place them in a dish and cover with plastic wrap. Let them cool for an hour.
5. Remove all the peels, and slice the vegetables (except the onion) into 1 ½-inch strips. Slice the onion into thin strips.
6. Place all the veggies in a mixing bowl, and stir in the garlic, salt, and red pepper flakes. Add the oil, and stir to coat.

Nutritional information
Calories: 327.2, Fat: 27.6 g, Protein: 3.6 g,
Carbs: 20.4 g, Sodium: 300 mg

Bread Recipes

Spanish White Bread

(*Pan Blanco,* or *Pan Basico*)

Spaniards eat a lot of bread, and it's usually white bread. This is the most common kind you'll find, and it will probably seem very familiar.

Serves: 16 - Prep time: 4 h - Cook time: 35–45 min

Ingredients
2 packets yeast
3 cups warm water
¼ cup sugar
1 teaspoon salt
8–9 cups all-purpose flour
¼ cup butter, melted

Directions
1. In a large mixing bowl, combine the yeast and sugar, and pour in the warm water. Cover, and let it stand for 5 minutes.
2. Add the salt and 6 cups of the flour. Mix well.
3. Add the melted butter and combine, and then add 2 more cups of flour. Mix well, and add more flour if necessary. The dough should be moist and soft, and not too stiff.
4. Flour a clean working space, and knead the dough for 10 minutes, until it is smooth and elastic. Place it in a greased bowl, cover, and let it rise until its size doubles.
5. Knead the dough briefly, and divide it into two loaves. Place it in greased pans, and let it rise again.
6. Preheat the oven to 350°F, and bake the loaves for 35–45 minutes. Let them cook before serving.

Nutritional information
Calories: 380, Fat: 2.9 g, Protein: 6.0 g,
Carbs: 47.1 g, Sodium: 165.8 mg

Spanish Bread Loaves (*Pan de Horno*)

Making fresh bread is always time consuming, and also worth it!

Serves: 10 - Prep time: 4 h - Cook time: 30 min

Ingredients
3 cups warm water
1 ½ tablespoons bread yeast
7 cups all-purpose flour
2 teaspoons salt
¼ cup olive oil

Directions
1. Stir the yeast into the warm water and set it aside to develop, about 10 minutes.
2. Sift the flour and salt into a large mixing bowl, and work in the oil using your fingertips.
3. Working slowly and still using your hands, mix in the yeast mixture until a firm dough is formed.
4. Transfer the dough to a floured work surface, and knead until it is smooth and elastic, 10–15 minutes.
5. Grease a bowl and put in the dough, turning to coat. Cover it with a damp kitchen towel, and set it aside to rise until it has doubled in size (1–2 hours, depending on your yeast and the temperature of the room).
6. Turn out the dough again onto a floured surface, and knead it again until all the air bubbles are removed. Return it to the bowl to rest for 15 minutes.
7. Preheat the oven to 450°F.
8. Cut the dough into little loaves or buns, according to your preference. Cut slits in the top, if desired. Allow the dough to rise in the pans for 30 minutes.
9. Bake for 30–50 minutes, until the loaves sound hollow when you knock on them.

Nutritional information
Calories: 328, Fat: 5.4 g, Protein: 8.4 g,
Carbs: 61.6 g, Sodium: 465 mg

Fluffy Buns (*Bunuelos de Viento*)

While the translation here is not perfect, it does convey the lovely texture of these sweet little dessert buns.

Makes: 24 - Prep time: 1 h 45 min - Cook time: 15–20 min

Ingredients
1 ¼ cups water
2 tablespoons butter
Zest of 1 lemon
2 teaspoons lemon juice
Pinch of salt
2 tablespoons granulated sugar
1 cup white flour
¼ teaspoon baking powder
4 eggs
3-4 cups vegetable oil for frying
Powdered sugar for dusting

Directions
1. In a small saucepan, combine the water, butter, lemon zest, lemon juice, salt, and sugar. Bring the mixture to a boil.
2. As soon as it boils, stir in the flour and baking powder. Stir briskly with a wooden spoon until the dough comes away from the sides of the pot. Set it aside to cool for 5–10 minutes.
3. One at a time, stir in the eggs. Mix until smooth, and then allow the batter to rest for 1 ½ hours.
4. Heat 2 inches of oil in a thick-bottomed pan. When it reaches 375°F, begin to drop rounded spoonfuls of the batter into the oil. Turn when they are golden on the bottom. When they're done they should float.

5. Remove the bunuelos to a paper towel to drain. While they are still hot, toss them with powdered sugar and serve.

Nutritional information
Calories: 70, Fat: 4.5 g, Protein: 1.6 g,
Carbs: 5.9 g, Sodium: 25.1 mg

Spanish Easter Bread (*Hornazo*)

Sausage and egg are baked into a loaf in this traditional food.

Serves: 10 - Prep time: 20 min plus 1 ½ h rising time –
Cook time: 35 min

Ingredients
5 cups bread flour
2 packets yeast
1 teaspoon salt
½ cup butter, cubed
1 ¾ cups water
1 egg, lightly beaten
1 egg yolk whisked with 1 tablespoon water, to glaze

For the filling:
8 ounces bacon, trimmed of excess fat and chopped
12 ounces chorizo, sliced half an inch thick
3 hard-boiled eggs, chopped

Directions
1. In a large mixing bowl, combine the flour, yeast, and salt.
2. In a saucepan over medium heat, melt the butter. Add the water and heat until it is warm, but not hot.
3. Add the water to the dry ingredients, together with the beaten egg and mix to form a dough.
4. Turn the dough out onto a floured surface, and knead for 10 minutes. Place it in a greased bowl in a warm place, and let it rise for an hour.
5. Cook the bacon and chorizo in a skillet until they start to crisp up. When they're ready, set them aside.
6. When the dough has risen, punch it down and knead it a few times. Spread it into a square 8" by 20".

7. Spread half the bacon and chorizo mixture along the center third of the dough. Use a bit of water to moisten the outer sides.
8. Fold one side of the dough over the filling, and top it with the remaining filling. Fold the other side over to cover, and press the edges to seal.
9. Line a baking sheet with parchment, and transfer the loaf to the sheet. Let it rise in a warm place, covered with a damp towel, for 30 minutes.
10. Preheat the oven to 375°F.
11. Using a sharp knife, cut diagonal slashes in the top of the loaf. Brush the top with egg wash.
12. Bake for 35–40 minutes, until it is nicely browned and sounds hollow when you tap on the bottom.

Nutritional information
Calories: 565, Fat: 29.0 g, Protein: 22.9 g,
Carbs: 50.6 g, Sodium: 908.7 mg

Corn Bread (*Boroña Asturiana*)

This dense and crispy loaf is sometimes filled with sausage, but try it plain first.

Serves: 8 - Prep time: 1 ½ h - Cook time: 40–45 min

Ingredients
5 cups corn flour
1 cup all-purpose flour
2 packets yeast
1 ½ teaspoons salt
1 ½ teaspoons sugar
⅓ cup extra virgin olive oil
2 cups warm water

Directions
1. Combine the corn flour, wheat flour, yeast, salt, and sugar in a mixing bowl (preferably the bowl of a stand mixer).
2. Add the oil, and begin to mix. Add the water gradually, and knead for 10 minutes, until a smooth, elastic ball is formed. Add a little more water if necessary.
3. Cover, and let it rest in a warm place for about an hour.
4. Preheat the oven to 400°F.
5. Knead the dough gently to remove any bubbles, and form it into a round loaf. Cut a cross on the top.
6. Bake for 40–45 minutes, or until the loaf sounds hollow when you tap on the bottom. Cool, and serve!

Nutritional information
Calories: 426, Fat: 9.5 g, Protein: 1.9 g,
Carbs: 83.7 g, Sodium: 436 mg

Dessert Recipes

Spanish King's Cake (*Roscón de reyes*)

This cake is traditionally served on January 6th, when it is said that the three wise men arrived to visit the baby Jesus.

Serves: 12 - Prep time: 2 ½ h - Cook time: 30 min

Ingredients
1 tablespoon active dry yeast
¼ cup warm water
¼ cup milk
¼ cup granulated sugar
¼ cup unsalted butter
½ teaspoon salt
¼ teaspoon ground mace
2 ½ cups all-purpose flour
1 egg
½ cup golden raisins
½ cup mixed candied fruit, chopped
¼ cup walnuts, chopped
1 tablespoon confectioners icing
2 tablespoons walnut halves
1 tablespoon candied fruit

Directions
1. Combine the yeast with the water, and set it aside to develop for about 5 minutes.
2. In a medium saucepan, combine the milk, sugar, butter, and salt. Heat to 115°F.
3. In a mixing bowl, combine the mace with 1 ½ cups of the flour, the warmed milk mixture, and egg. Mix well.
4. Add the raisins, candied fruit, and chopped walnuts. Add enough flour to form a soft dough, and knead for about 10 minutes, until soft and elastic.

5. Grease a bowl and put in the dough, turning to coat. Let it rise until it is doubled in size, about 1 ½ hours.
6. Punch down the dough and roll it out into two 20-inch "ropes." Twist them together, and arrange them on a cookie sheet. Cover, and let it rise for one hour.
7. Preheat the oven to 350°F, and bake for 30 minutes.
8. Let the cake cool, and then frost it with the icing and decorate it with the remaining walnuts and candied fruit.

Nutritional information
Calories: 222, Fat: 6.3 g, Protein: 3.9 g,
Carbs: 39 g, Sodium: 145.4 mg

Churros

No discussion of Spanish desserts would be complete without churros, the famous street food from Madrid.

Serves: 4 - Prep time: 15 min - Cook time: 5 min

Ingredients
1 cup water
3 tablespoons granulated sugar
½ teaspoon salt
2 tablespoons butter
1 cup all-purpose flour
3–4 cups oil, for frying
½ cup granulated sugar
1 teaspoon cinnamon

Directions
1. In a saucepan over medium heat, combine the water with 3 tablespoons sugar, salt, and butter. Bring it to a boil.
2. As soon as it boils, stir in the flour. Mix until it forms a ball.
3. Place the dough into a pastry bag and secure the 1/4-inch star tip.
4. Heat the oil to 375°F, and set out a plate lined with paper towel.
5. Combine ½ cup of sugar with the cinnamon in a bowl.
6. Pipe strips of batter into the oil and fry until golden. Using a slotted spoon, remove them to the paper towel.
7. While they are still hot, coat them with cinnamon sugar and serve fresh!

Nutritional information
Calories: 460, Fat: 34.4 g, Protein: 2.2 g,
Carbs: 38.1 g, Sodium: 195.3 mg

Crema Catalana

Crema Catalana is Spain's answer to crème brulée, and it's simpler to make than the French version!

Serves: 6 - Prep time: 10 min plus 4 h cooling time - Cook time: 10 min

Ingredients
2 ½ cups whole milk
1 thick slice of peel from a lemon and an orange (the whole peel, not just the zest)
1 cinnamon stick
5 large egg yolks
½ cup superfine sugar
2 tablespoons cornstarch, dissolved in 1 tablespoon water
Additional sugar to caramelize on top

Directions
1. Place the milk in a medium saucepan together with the fruit peels and the cinnamon stick, and heat it slowly over medium heat until it boils.
2. Beat the egg yolks well with the sugar, and stir in the dissolved cornstarch.
3. Remove the fruit peels and the cinnamon stick from the milk, and reduce the heat to minimum.
4. Slowly add the egg mixture to the hot milk, whisking constantly so the eggs don't scramble. Stir constantly until the pudding thickens.
5. Pour the mixture into ramekins. Allow them to cool, and then refrigerate them for 4 hours (or overnight)
6. Before serving, sprinkle a thin layer of sugar on top of the custard, and caramelize it with a kitchen torch.

Nutritional information
Calories: 182, Fat: 7.1 g, Protein: 5.6 g,
Carbs: 24.5 g, Sodium: 56.9 g

Spanish Cream Pastry (*Miguelitos*)

These look like they're hard to make, but they're not. Give them a try!

Makes: 18 - Prep time: 15 min plus cooling time –
Cook time: 15 min

Ingredients
2 packages frozen puff pastry, thawed
1 egg, beaten
2 cups whole milk, divided
⅓ cup white sugar
3 egg yolks
¼ cup cornstarch
½ teaspoon cinnamon
½ teaspoon vanilla extract
Zest of half a lemon
Icing sugar for dusting

Directions
1. Preheat the oven to 375°F.
2. Roll out the pastry to ⅛-inch thickness, and cut it into 3" squares.
3. Paint the squares with the beaten egg, and bake until they are golden brown. Set them aside to cool.
4. Heat half the milk in a saucepan until it is almost boiling.
5. In a bowl, combine the egg yolks with the sugar until smooth. Stir in the cornstarch (you can dissolve it in a splash of milk first to avoid lumps), cinnamon, vanilla, and lemon zest. Stir in the remaining milk.
6. Slowly add the cold milk mixture to the hot milk, whisking constantly. Cook over medium low heat until it is very thick. Set it aside to cool slightly.

7. Gently separate the cooked puffed pastry sheets, top layer from bottom.
8. Spread the custard filling on the bottom layer, and cover it with the top.
9. Dust with icing sugar, and serve cool.

Nutritional information

Calories: 190, Fat: 11.5 g, Protein: 3.5 g,
Carbs: 18.2 g, Sodium: 81.6 g

Spanish Almond Cake (*Tarta de Santiago*)

This citrusy almond cake dates back to the middle ages and can be found in many places, especially Galicia, where it is said to have originated.

Serves: 6 - Prep time: 5 min - Cook time: 40 min

Ingredients
2 cups ground almonds
1 cup caster sugar
¾ teaspoon ground cinnamon
Zest of 1 lemon, grated
Pinch of salt
4 large eggs
icing sugar for dusting

Directions
1. Preheat the oven to 350°F. Cut parchment to fit the bottom of a 8" springform pan, and spray it with cooking spray.
2. In a mixing bowl, combine the almonds, sugar, cinnamon, lemon zest, and salt. Beat in the eggs one at a time.
3. Bake for 40 minutes, or until a toothpick inserted in the center comes out clean. Cool the cake in the pan.
4. When it is cool, dust the top with icing sugar, and serve.

Nutritional information
Calories: 342, Fat: 21.9 g, Protein: 12.2 g,
Carbs: 28.6 g, Sodium: 73.3 g

Spanish Eggy Bread (*Torrijas*)

Similar to French toast but with a lemon twist, *Torrijas* are another tasty and inexpensive dish to prepare.

Serves: 5 - Prep time: 10 min - Cook time: 20 min

Ingredients
1 stale baguette (or loaf of French bread)
4 cups milk
2 tablespoons sugar
1 cinnamon stick
Peel of 1 lemon
2 eggs
Oil for frying
Cinnamon sugar, for dusting

Directions
1. Slice the bread into 2-inch slices, and set it aside.
2. In a saucepan, heat the milk. Stir in the sugar, and add the cinnamon stick and lemon peel. Heat, stirring often, for 5–10 minutes, but don't allow it to boil.
3. Remove the saucepan from the heat and allow it to cool for a few minutes.
4. In a medium-sized bowl, beat the eggs.
5. Heat 1 inch of oil in a skillet.
6. Dip the bread slices into the milk until they are soaked through, and then into the beaten egg. Fry them in the hot oil on one side until browned, and then cook on the other side.
7. Drain the bread slices on a piece of paper towel, and sprinkle them with cinnamon sugar while they're still hot.

Nutritional information
Calories: 381, Fat: 12.1 g, Protein: 1 g,
Carbs: 28.6 g, Sodium: 73.3 g

Recipe Index

Also by Sarah Spencer

  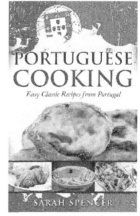

Easy and Healthy Ramen Noodle Bowl Recipes

SARAH SPENCER

SARAH SPENCER

CHINESE COOKING

FAVORITE CHINESE TAKEOUT RECIPES

TACOS

Best Homemade Taco Recipes from Breakfast Tacos to Street Tacos and Dessert Tacos

SARAH SPENCER

BEST BACKYARD BBQ RECIPES

From Around the World

100 QUICK AND EASY GRILLING RECIPES

SARAH SPENCER

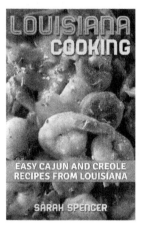

LOUISIANA COOKING

EASY CAJUN AND CREOLE RECIPES FROM LOUISIANA

SARAH SPENCER

SPICE IT UP!

THE BEST SPICE MIXING RECIPES FROM AROUND THE WORLD

SARAH SPENCER

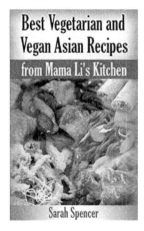

Best Vegetarian and Vegan Asian Recipes

from Mama Li's Kitchen

Sarah Spencer

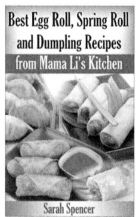

Best Egg Roll, Spring Roll and Dumpling Recipes

from Mama Li's Kitchen

Sarah Spencer

Best Chinese Take-Out Recipes

from Mama Li's Kitchen

Sarah Spencer

Appendix - Cooking Conversion Charts

1. Measuring Equivalent Chart

Type	Imperial	Imperial	Metric
Weight	1 dry ounce		28g
	1 pound	16 dry ounces	0.45 kg
Volume	1 teaspoon		5 ml
	1 dessert spoon	2 teaspoons	10 ml
	1 tablespoon	3 teaspoons	15 ml
	1 Australian tablespoon	4 teaspoons	20 ml
	1 fluid ounce	2 tablespoons	30 ml
	1 cup	16 tablespoons	240 ml
	1 cup	8 fluid ounces	240 ml
	1 pint	2 cups	470 ml
	1 quart	2 pints	0.95 l
	1 gallon	4 quarts	3.8 l
Length	1 inch		2.54 cm

* Numbers are rounded to the closest equivalent

2. Oven Temperature Equivalent Chart

Fahrenheit (°F)	Celsius (°C)	Gas Mark
220	100	
225	110	1/4
250	120	1/2
275	140	1
300	150	2
325	160	3
350	180	4
375	190	5
400	200	6
425	220	7
450	230	8
475	250	9
500	260	

*   Celsius (°C) = T (°F)-32] * 5/9

**   Fahrenheit (°F) = T (°C) * 9/5 + 32

*** Numbers are rounded to the closest equivalent

Printed in Great Britain
by Amazon

82639630R00068